1

Dreaming Rhythms
Despertando silencios

Pandora Lobo Estepario Productions™
Editors

Dreaming Rhythms
Despertando silencios

Carmen Bardeguez-Brown

DEDICATION

I want to dedicate this book to my family. Our love has helped us
navigate our life journey with grace, laughter and hope.
Thank you for the lessons.

ACKNOWLEDGMENTS

There are so many people that I need to give thanks for supporting my journey as a poet. My family, my dear son Hector and my beloved husband and partner, Raul. I know that you are still watching over me. Steve Cannon, Bob Holman, Steve Roach, Lois Griffin and Miguel Algarin for their support in the early 1990s at the Nuyorican Poets Café and the Stoop at Steve's house. Sandra Maria Estevez and Nancy Mercado for their constant reminder that I am a member of the Nuyorican tradition. Papoleto Melendez for his passion. Ra Araya for his support. Woman Writers in Bloom workshops lead by Juliet Howard. The series rescue me when I was lost. Oya Bisi for her kindness and inspiration. Capicu for their passion, love and support. Xanath Caraza for guiding me to Miguel at Pandora Lobo Estepario. Finally, Miguel thank you for believing in my voice and the message of my words.

Carmen Bardeguez-Brown

PRÓLOGO

Carmen Bardeguez-Brown es poeta y educadora de Puerto Rico y residente de la ciudad de Nueva York. En los noventas se incorporó a la escena poética debutando en el conocido Nuyorican Poets Café bajo la tutela de Bob Holman, Louis Griffith, Miguel Algarin y Keith Roach. Fue miembro del taller literario Stoop dirigido por Steven Cannon y Bob Holman.

Parte del trabajo de Carmen Bardeguez-Brown ha sido documentado en Latino Poets in the United States. Un documental producido por Ray Santiesteban, donde la reconocen como uno de los miembros fundadores del movimiento poético The Nuyorican Poets Café a la par de Pedro Pietri y Willie Perdomo.

Bardeguez-Brown ha participado, entre otros festivales, en The New York Poetry Festival en Governors Island, The Bowery Poetry Club, Sarah Lawrence College Poetry Reading series, Bronx Music Heritage Center y The Caribbean Cultural Theater Literary Festival.

También es parte de la exhibición itinerante Homenaje, curada por Ricardo Muñiz y adquirida por el Center of Puerto Rican Studies de Hunter College en la ciudad de Nueva York. Su poesía ha sido antologada en Afro Latino Poetry y, por varios años, ha sido miembro activo del taller de poesía Woman Writers in Bloom. Su primer poemario es Straight from the Drums: Al ritmo del tambor, su segundo poemario es Dreaming Rythms.

La poesía de Carmen encapsula el ritmo afropoético del Caribe. Su poesía es para ser leída en voz alta y para ser dramatizada. Sus sílabas invitan al lector a viajar con ella desde el Bronx a Puerto Rico y de vuelta. El ritmo del tambor está presente en cada poema e invita a alzar la voz mientras el cuerpo vibra para honrar a los ancestros, que llegaron forzados desde África, y que lograron traspasar las creencias religiosas a las nuevas generaciones. Deidades como Shangó y Obalatá emergen de los versos de Bardeguez-Brown.

Creando sonidos
Que Obalatá y Shagó bailaron
¡Ay! Salseros del ayer
Sáquenme
Los sonidos
Y el ¡ay, bendito!
En la ciudad de Babel

En muchos de sus poemas, Carmen usa poesía concreta e invita al lector tanto a un viaje visual como literario. Juega con las mayúsculas, las negritas, lo signos de puntuación, los tipos de letra y los espacios. Como consecuencia transforma cada página en un universo lúdico.

El Bronx
THE BRONX
Suéñame en dos
Dos por dos
Ámame hoy
Timbales
Tócame
ARRIBA Y A
B
A
J
O

En su poesía hay una combinación natural entre el español y el inglés; reflejando la historia lingüística de Puerto Rico en sus versos y su propia historia de migración desde la isla a Nueva York. Mezcla la lengua del Bardo

Rutgers
Profesor emeritus
Canon
Nixing
Nueva palabra
Española
Inglés
Spanglish

NuYorican
Nuyorriquense
Español
Coloreando con
El inglés de la clase trabajadora
En el Lower East Side
Loisa
Loisa…ida
Lower East Side

No solo la historia lingüística sino la musical y literaria son los
orígenes del ritmo en los poemas de Carmen. Hace un esfuerzo
consciente y lo comparte con los lectores. En su poesía incorpora
a diferentes poetas y escritores, Miguel Algarín, Lorca, entre otros;
y músicos puertorriqueños que radican o radicaron en la ciudad de
Nueva York.

Tú me diste tu bendición
Tus compañeros
Pedro, Sandra, Papoleto, Piñero y Nancy
Enriquecieron el legado de
Chaucer
Cervantes
Pales y Lorca
Y tú

Miguel
Con tu permiso y bendición
Quiero celebrarte

Sus poemas también son de comentario social, resaltan la negritud
puertorriqueña en Nueva York. Sus versos hablan de las clases
sociales en esa urbe neoyorquina, de las carencias y de la riqueza
que hay, día a día, en las calles: los sonidos, las voces diversas, el
uso del inglés y español por los Boricuas; pero tampoco olvida a la
isla de Puerto Rico y, como poeta, nos recuerda sus aromas, sus
colores, sus sabores y los sueños, que trajo consigo misma, y que
ahora los escribe desde un escritorio en el Bronx.

El Cross County Express
Nos dividió
Mientras el Caribe
Nos bautizó
Y sé que estoy aquí en Nuyol
Pero
No es Nuyol
Es El Bronx
The Bronx
Da'Bronx
El South Bronx

Tuve el placer de haber conocido a Carmen Bardeguez-Brown en Brooklyn Workshop Gallery, de Martine Bisagni, en un taller organizado, en noviembre de 2014, por Juliet P. Howard para Women Writers in Bloom.

Xánath Caraza, Writer-in-Residence, WCC, NY
Kansas City, MO, 2017

Dreaming Rythms

Despertando Silencios

POEMS

Única

Iam
Amapolas
Chrysanthemums
Guanábana
And the tender meat of ripe mangoes.
My skin has bathe in crimson roses
And birth life
In a jungle
Of impossibilities.
This body has
Rebirth scars
That lacerated the souls of thousands of warriors
Like an amazon
I fought my right
To caress my wounds
And seed the pain
In kisses
Engulf in the aroma of orchids.

I breathe cinnamon
&
Acerola
Sweet coconut milk travels through my veins.

Iam
Spicy peppers
Marinated in the warm
Sweet oil
Of ancient olives.

I am rhythms
Of

Conga
Timbales
Bongos and clave
Remeneando
Manos
Hombros
Piernas
Caderas
Muslos

Ancient movements
Encrypted
In every cellular DNA strand.
Yemaya is my mother

But
My spirit is thunder.

I create universes
One at a time.

I am the daughter
Sister
Grandmother
Lover
Of every dream
At any time.

I am what I am

A unique
And
Extraordinary
Woman.

Skin

The greatest camouflage of all
A web of Hearts
Blood
veins
Synchronistically
Singing
The rhythms
of
The soul.

Time

Is but a pause in your imagination
At all times in every moment
We are
Past
Future
Present
And
then
This moment
Exhale
eternity
In a solemn breath.

Cosmic Reality

We are weave in a basket of illusions
In waves
And we think life is like a straight arrow
Straight and firm
But
in the wisdom of our hearts
We know
That one is forever
In everything
and everything is one
In
love.

Remembrance

Part 1

Babalu
 Ache
     Orishas
 Bembete
 Ay denme la porción
         Orischas
 Swirl Ache
     Asfalto bembeando
   Candomble candombeando
   Sirenas
       Dance ando
 Los sueños
 Penetrando
         Dance ando
 Enchanted
 souls

 Embrújenme
 Ay con el Son
 Come
     S
     W
       I
         R
         L
             Ache
 Orischas
       swirl
             Ache
 Orischas
 swirl
         Ache, Ache, Ache.

Part 2

To Understand

You need to taste
Memories of salt and water
Blood
Chains
D
  R
    O
     W
       N
      I
        N
         G
In the Middle of the Ocean
A Christian boat
Foreign tongues
Memories
Sounds
Despair swallow souls
Yemaya
Yemaya
Llévame
Yemaya.

Parte 3

Llena de cadenas
Soledades muertas
El silencio de mil años
Aumenta
El vaivén de las olas
Acarician los calientes sueños
De un Mundo lejano
El vaivén
Va y Viene
El vaivén
 Va
Va y ven
Va y ven
Viene
Encrespado en amapolas
Solas
Amapolas Solas
Escuchando las olas.

Part 4

I cry
No mas
Silences
In the tumultuous morning of desires
 Dreaming
Castañuelas

    Noche eterna.

Señora

Tun   Tun
Pasa y grifería
Tun ca tun tun
In the city
Babel
Extasieria
Run ca tun tun
Negra ven
Cobíjame del hierro
Negra
        Rumbanbeame
        Del dream
        Tun tun
        No tengo sueño
        Run ca tun
Pasiones
Runcatuntun
Tus eyes
Tun ca tun pa
Tus ojos
        Eterna
        Melancholia
            Hundreds of tuns
            Masked my pain
                        Negra
                Run Ta
Tun tun ca pa
Your eyes
Eternal
Melancholia
Hundreds of tuns
Masked my pain

Negra

Run ta

Tantanea

In your dreams

Despiértame del sueño

My tears

Tun Tun ca

Make love to my canto

Tun tun ca ta

Yemaya

Runcatunta

Báñame ya

Yemaya

Ahora

Ya

Ahhhhhhhh

  Báñame toda

Rumbanbeame

Cancanéame

Tunantéame

Yemayeame

Remenéame

Ven

Y

Tómame

Señora.

Bongocero's Song

Acumba Cumba
Cumbanchero
A Bongo Bongo
 Bongocero
¿Dónde están?
Machito
 Benny
 Ismael
Suenen el African bembe
Celia
 Tito
Hector
Denme agua
Que me muero
Tengo sed
Bembe
Rumba
 Requete
Suénamelo bien
Dance with Me Afro-Cuban
Bongocero del ayer
Bañame en Yemaya
Música de Obatala
Benbeteame en tu verdad
Acumba
Rumba
Piernas
Culos
Negruras
Tambor
Cumbanchero scratch me deep
Bembe suénamelo así

Cumba
Cumba
Rumba

Rumba
Cumba
Tumba

Sensations
Libations
Lamentos

Bongocero
Ton Ton
Orgasméame
Con tu son
Consúmate
Tambor
Troquetéame
Bongo
Tambor
trocoto
Bongocéame
Acumbánbame
Acumbánbame
Acumbánbame.

Pachanga Memoirs

Love is a splendor thing
Me dijo mamacita
You know what I mean?
She said that men are weird
" They stick it like thunder
And in a flash disappear."
She met my father in
El Palladium
Bailando Pachanga y Charanga
con Pacheco
And in between the sones
Se Fueron
charangueando
Cha Cha Cha
(do you want to know el resto)?
She said Papa era handsome
Un negro bonito
Tu sabes un mulato
Que al oir.
Las congas
Tru Cu tun ca ta
Le salia lo Africano
They dance Charanga,Pachanga
Se pasaban Charangueando
But in one of those sonetes
My papa se fue.
Trucuteando

E L   BRONX

Songo
Songo
  Dreaming in the

Asphalt   Jungle
Conga
Rythms
In the midst of the
Urban LULLUBY

El Bronx
THE BRONX
Sonéame en dos
Two for two
Love me NOW
Timbales
Touching ME
UP AND D
              O
                W
                  N
Hmmmmmmmmmm
Sonéame
congonéame
Así, así
Bamboléame
Muslos y piernas
remenéame
Tito

me toca

Caliente
Y Baretto
Me hace sudar la frente

En PS. 52
Los musicos gozaron
Creating Sounds
Que Obatala Y Shango Bailaron
Ay Salseros del ayer
Saquenme
Los sounds
Y el ay Bendito
En la ciudad de Babel

El Cross County Express
Nos Dividio
While the Caribbean
Nos Bautizó
Y sé que estoy aquí en Nuyol
But
Is not Nuyol
Is The Bronx
Da' Bronx
El south Bronx
El South Bronx of theYankee Stadium of 73'
Of the Mambo
Of the streets
Of the dreams left behind
 in a suitcase
Guardados
En el closet
Hasta el Próximo viaje
Yes,
The Next trip
Because, tu sabes

Puerto Ricans are here
And There
But no
We are here

in Da' Bronx

Songoneando

In Da' Bronx

Guaracheando

In Da' Bronx

Sandongueando

In Da' Bronx

Salseando
Congoneando
Soneando
We are here
You hear me World!!!!!!!!!!!!!!
We are here to stay.

Dislocations
Pensando en Puerto Rico

The smell of alelí
Remembers a distant future
Of coco y pasteles
Yuca,ñame y café con leche
Aromatic memoirs
Chicharones de Bayamón

Viajando por la carretera número 2
Drinking piraguas en el Bronx
Memoirs of salt
Sea
Caña y piña
Translated in millions of taste
Sinsabores amargos
And the lullaby of a pitirre
Cantico del coquí
Frozen in giant mirrors
Of voices

Tasting piñones
Y arroz con dulce sin pasas.

Oye Miguel
To Miguel Algarín

¿Qué pasa papa?
Celebrating your cumpleaños
Your birth
Birth
Day
As in giving birth
Nacimiento
 Movimiento
    voices
Cadencias de mambo y conga
Rumba y timbales
Songo
Y Bemba
Ayyyyyyy
Menéamelo bien
Mixing the language of the Bard
Rutgers
Professor emeritus
Canon
 Nixing
A new lexicon
Española
English
Spanglish
NuYorican
Spanish
Coloreado con
Working class English language
En el Lower East Side
Loisa
Loisa....ida

Lower east side
Se convirtió en
Loisaida
Porque
Aquí estamos
Con las credenciales of
One hundred years of coloniaje
1898
1917
Our language is written in blood
El chef del language atribulado
Creating sounds
Of us
For us
By us
Cooking mofongo of the Puerto Rican soul
Puerto Rican
Nuyorican
Sancocho y salsa
Creating a sacred place
To celebrate our cultures
Embracing the universal
Ay Bendito
Miguelito
Tu visión acurruco
Mi imaginación
Tú me distes tu bendición
Your cooking partners
Pedro, Sandra, Papoleto, Piñero y Nancy
Enriched the legacy of
Chaucer
Cervantes
Pales y Lorca
Y tú

Miguel

Con tu permiso y bendición
Quiero celebrarte
Como padre de un movimiento
You show us el soneo universal
Rumbeando palabras
Sonéando
Nuestra esencia en la virtud del poema.

En la esquina
   For Pedro Pietri

El pan nuestro de cada día
Líbranos hoy de
Silencios
Castrados
Senses
Armed in still life images
Jesús
Jesucristo
Boom
Boom
Y no es de conga
La Agúja se tripio
En el vaivén del son
Respirando
Breathing death
Another corpse
Yes
fulano
  died
     yesterday
Right after beating up Ramona
Rafael's daughter
The same girl
That dropped from school
Dropped from life
Si
La misma que aborto mañana
Añorando
La Esperanza
Incierta

Balbuceante
Semejante a soledades
Salpicadas de tristeza
Música brava

Bailando al son de Miranda
Amaneciéndonos todos
En Los "rufos"
Aguardiente
Calor
Embriagados
En sudor
Reza
Reza
A ver si nos escucha
Reza reza
And ask for the Landlord
To give us a break
Tell the kids to Open the hydrant
Maybe
El agua nos Bautiza
Y el well fare no da
Así que voy a jugar la bolita
Me voy a la bodega
A ver si nos pegamos
Y no es a lavar los platos
Reza reza y vete al novenario
Yo me voy a comprar cerveza
A lo mejor un domino
Y a hablar con Los muchachos.

Rican Issues

Say **What?**

Could you please, Pleaseeeeeeeeee repeat
Did you said:" Molleta?
    Prieta?
    Morena?
  Ohh African!
Hmmmmm, **Soy Puertoriqueña.**

Yes, **P**uertorican.

That I don't look **W**hat ?

Oh, I guess I don't look cafe con leche

mancha de plátano
Mulata,
high yellow
grifa
By the way

I did not know that there was a Puerto Rican look.
And, what exactly is that?
That I just look more what?
Well

¿Y Tu abuela donde Esta?

I should said abuela, tío, tia, y todo el barrio
Let me tell you something

For your information
Most Ricans are a mixed of Africans, Spaniards and
Native Americans called Tainos
By the way no one has seen a Taino in the last 500
years.
So exactly... You know what that means

My   English is covered with spices

Spices from theCaribbean

Spices that you might find Strange
Because you were born in this cold fast food mall of a
country

Where Spanish is a foreign word
That you are ashamed to learn
And when you try
Is not there
Only mumbles of a murmur
Susurando el olvido

A regañadientes

Pretendiendo

Escondiendo la vergüenza.

You remember Puerto Rico on the 2nd Sunday of every
June
When everybody is suddenly proud to be Puerto Rican.

No the word is Boricua

Boricuas here, Boricuas there, Boricuas everywhere

And everyone waves the flags
The flags that they don't even understand
And no one knows why they are here.

Yes HERE **N**ow
Do you Know?

why your parents or grandparents, vinieron aquí?

¿De qué Pueblo?

¿Cuándo te bañastes en las aguas calientes del Caribe?
Better yet
Do you really know that…?
We all came from the motherland
Africa

Even the Spanish people that came with **Colón,**
Columbus
However you want to say it
Lived 700 hundred years under the **Moors.**
You heard that right.
The moors as in Arabs as in black Arabs
SO … in other words
Not only I
But **we**
Have over 500 years of African mestizaje
The so called "white people that everyone is so proud of"

As in "my grand parents are from Spain
Well if they are...
They
Too   have **negrITOs** in them.

26

Remember the **Gitanos**

But that is another story…

Getting back to the **Boricua's issue**

   What history do you know?

Ever heard of
Agueybana
Albizu Campos
Pales Matos
Rafael Betances
Arturo Shomburg
Francisco Oller
Julia De Burgos
Rafael Hernández
Segundo Ruiz Belvis
Enrique Laguerre
Mariana Bracetti
Pedro Pietri

Still havING problems figuring me out?

Or is it that you just don't know
Who you are?

Summer Poem

I was going to write my summer poem
    When...
The rhythms of the streets
The smell of
Alcapurrias
        bacalaítos and burning burgers
Call me out!
I walk outside and see
El agua corriendo como un rio
        Fire hydrants
       baptizing everyone
      Our communal fountain
        Because
     We are all equal
   Living the misery of this heat

This suffocating
       heat of the asphalt jungle
     Sweating
     Sweating
     Sweating
   Dios mio,que Calor!
    Y las mamis
Showing everything off
    Flip flap
    Flip flap
Meneando those big thights
Those big thights that are not ashame
To seek shelter from the smoldering heat
In the warm breeze of a man's gaze
But hey
This is Nuyol

Yes,
　　Nuyol
Of the short short pants
Of the big big breasts hanging effortlessly
In some kind of physical impossibility in a tight shirt.
　　Nuyol of the congas
Rhythms in Crotona park
Of Dominican fans paying Yankee tickets with their
lunch and dinner money
Of the Puerto Rican day parade
　　　Of Bushwick
　　　the Heights
　　　El Barrio
　　　Da Bronx
　　This is Nuyol
　Nuyol en ESPAÑOL.

La Santa Sede

Invested in Centuries of illusions
Repressed sperms crucify vaginas
Thousands of requiems
Catapulted in Ave Marías
Idolatría infinita
Inmaculadas
En el umbral de la nada
Avergonzadas
Angustiadas
Desoladas
Solas
Senses
Feels
left
out.

Soneo en dos
Song for two (But one is missing)

It was fast
As fast as an eternal glimpse of hell
As powerful as the love that is not there
As deep as a wound with no scars

canela
skin
negra
flor
tierno capullo en flor
Out
inside

pa'fuera

canela
pena
In side

pa'fuera

canela
pena

de adentro pa'fuera
FIGHT
piernas y muslos
Tight
Fist
piernas
La Noche Negra
pena, nena

miss
missing
missing song
mi son
mi historia
mistoria
ahora
ORA
PRAY
ahora añora
vacaciones caribeñas
Pena, nena
SON
Some song
song for dos
missing one
one is fighting
but is two
But is one
One is fighting
FIGHT
son de pena
llora nena
FIGHT LA PENA
PELEA
FIGHT LA PELEA
llora
llora
Cry
some more some more
song for dos
but is one
fighting
no more
no more

Ahora
Llora
Ahora llora nena.

Collection

For Saartjie Baartman

Rage
Venus
Clitoris Observed
Clip clitoris clip
Fashion bird
Clitoris clip
Pubic public
Derriere
Culo publico
Pussy
Pubic public pussy
Mama mama mamacita
Negra negra negrita
Morenita

Trigueña
Noir
La Negra
Bemba
Bembéando
Dancéando
Cottonéando
Cut
Cotton cotton
Cut
Vulva
Dancéa
Banboléa
Out of your vulva
Negra retumba
La negra Tumba
Miradas Turbias

Corta la vulva
Cotton cotton cut
Azúcar melao tristezas
Cotton cotton cut
In pieces
Clitoris clip
Negra
Las calles
Museum of
Man-kind
Clitoris clip
Mama mama mamacita
Morena
Negra
Negrita
Culo africano
Venus bembéando
Sangrando
In the cage
RAGE
COTTON COTTON CUT
CUT
REVIENTA
BEMBA
LA VENUS NEGRA.

Declaración de independencia
De una mujer menopaúsica

Este poema no tiene traducción
Para todos los que creen que esto es una
democracia
Hmmmmmm...
 tu madre te parió
 te dio la vida para que
Vieras y vivieras con tus propios ojos
La pendeja que es esto que se llama vida
Porque naces envuelto en sangre y te mueres
llena de mierda.
Y entre sol y sol
Te enamoras y crees que eres feliz y después
cuando crees que ya lo tienes todo
Resuelto
te salen las canas
Your breast starts to fall down
And your derrière enlarge to a gargantuan size
Y te sientes joven pero ya no lo eres
Aunque te pintes el pelo las canas de allá abajo no
se pueden pintar por que sino
sí que tenemos problemas
Pues como iba diciendo.
Esta es mi declaración de independencia.
Iam done with pretensions.
> Porque la vida es muy corta y mis nalgas
> siguen creciendo
> And my breast keep falling past my stomach.

Así que de ahora en adelante
Voy a hacer lo que me da la gana
Y a el que no le guste
pues
Goodbye.

Bliss

I drink nectar of petals and querubines
dreaming
dancing
bowing
I drink nectar of petals and querubines
dreaming
dancing
bowing
moving circles
sunsets and mornings
glowing winds caressing unknown vistas
I drink nectar of petals and querubines
dreaming
dancing
 breathing
your love
in
and
out
sunsets and mornings
moving circles
cosmic karma
 dancing
drinking nectar of petals and querubines
bowing.

El Amor de la Paloma

Eat me slowly
Como pan caliente
Drink me
Quietly
Como agua bendita
Desliza tu pasión como la lava
Mientras reventamos
En un delirio de Amor eterno.

Conjugations

We are verbs searching for meaning
In the vast ocean of existence.
You
I
We
Us
Intertwine in hibiscus
roses
Amapolas
And
Flamboyan
We are shadows of love
Burned in the ashes of sorrow.
Us
We
You
I

Dance in circles
Smelling earth and corpses.
We are love awaiting to feel.
We are pain
Forgiving to cry.
And
You
I
We
Us
Are
crystals
Capullos congelados

Encrypted
Quietly
Murmuring
For the door of wisdom
To open our heart.

Stardust

*We are grains of
eternity
Dancing with the stars.*

Tus ojos

Te siento en mi corazón
Tu pasión
Tus palabras
Y duermo en tu sonrisa
Mientras sueño tu mirada.

Super Nova

Your death
blessed my birth
In
melodic explosions
Orchestrated
in gravitational echoes
Ancient
Sounds
Burping existence
In a symphony
Of
Colors
Awaiting
For us
To see.

Simple Math

Numbers and love sometimes equal
passion.
   If I add the sum of the burning desire that I
see in your eyes.
        To the energy of my trembles when u
touch me.
   The product of our interaction explodes in a
balanced passionate.
   Equation.

Distancia

No entiendo el castigo de tu mirada
Y la dureza de tu corazón
Sólo sé que te extraño
Y mi amor se seca en un desierto marchito
Lleno de soledad.

Tiempo

Eres fugaz como aroma de amapolas
como el ave que suspira llegar al arco iris de la
nada
como gaviota aventurera
como hormiga eficaz
como locura
como el perro que espera
como el amor perdido
como la lucha
como la muerte
como el olor a sexo
como el orgasmo que esperas
como el amor

como el adiós

como el amigo
como la sonrisa de tus hijos
como el hogar perdido
como el encuentro infinito
como la risa

como la pasión

como la inercia de besos en espera
como la lluvia
como el recuerdo
como la tarde que espere el encuentro
como el aliento
como el suspiro
como el pecado

como el olvido

como saciarme de tu olor y beberte hasta
desfallecer
como hiedra
como el deseo de tenerte entre mis piernas
como la vida
como la espera
como el Amor
Envuelto en sal y enlazado en hiedra.

Momento

Agua perdida
en el rio de la esperanza
aliento sediento
Que cabalga
del amor
al olvido

sueño inocente

espiga naciente
hacia ti ruego
desde ti lloro
laberintos secos
transformados
en olas del comienzo.

Tarde

Una canción y comienzas a recordar
Emociones de una época
La soledad
La angustia
La Inseguridad
Y me dio tanta pena
Una pena tan profunda
Que no la podía medir
Pues
no existe
Es como un equilibrio de pasiones
Que recorren todo un torbellino
De memorias
Y me dio una tristeza
Pero
Es la tristeza que no se tiene
De una felicidad que se esconde
En la memoria de un closet
Cubierto de telarañas
Y el corazón

Es el eslabón que detiene el tiempo

Y con cada suspiro
El momento de la creación
Es un recuerdo.

La Espera

Si supieras como el recuerdo de tu voz me estremece
Si supieras lo que mi corazón
Ahora siente
Si supieras los latidos cálidos
Si anhelaras
Los suspiros mágicos
Estarías mi amor
Ahora a mi lado

¿Qué es lo que pasa corazón?

¿Qué ya no quieres mi pasión?

Sueño contigo
Y no te tengo a mi lado
Momentos mágicos
De ayer
Que al corazón
Me hacen creer
Quizás mañana
Te tenga yo a mi
Lado
Corazón.

Intermitente

Cuento de hadas
Serpientes y cascabeles
Me encuentro
En un mundo de lamentos
Acariciando segundos en desvelo
Anhelando suspiros
Como un cisne
Buscando el olvido
Cuantas veces
Atravesé las cortinas de un mundo vivido
En un mar infinito
Más la quebrada se seco
Y tengo sed de nadar
Y veo ríos, lagos y océanos
Me pregunto
¿A cuál iré a nadar?

Cartografía

Soy
un mapa infinito
De caricias y te quieros
Soy el agua
Que sacia tus deseos
Soy tu Amor
Soy tu anhelo
Soy la esperanza perdida
De un Amor pasajero
Soy el mapa de tus deseos
Soy el mapa de tus deseos.

BURNING
For the Rolling Stones

Come and taste
 the oldest desire in the world
Its been around for a long time
creeping through every living heart
breaking rules
conventions
 repression
burning passions
  pain
Iam as old as creation
 do you guess my name?
fallen angels carved their lust in the bosom of fire
women were burned for their power
Cleopatra conquered worlds
feverish
 melancholic
lustily
 moaning
Eve betrayed us
always
 wanting
 more
mas
 more
give give
give me
 more
Salomon's songs
Cantar de los cantares
Love
Lust
Amor

Helen
destroyed
Troy
Romeo drank
Poison
Juliet stabbed
Her heart
call my name

ven acá

ven acá

passionS
desires
give me more
more
and then again
is just
burning
burning
crimes committed
Samson & Delilah
Brando
Dean
Marilyn
everyone wants
her bliss
millions fake her
make me
come
call
what is my name?
call
call me

ven acá

twisting
rhythms
 playing
Clinton
Lewinsky
temptation
seduction
pleasure
 moon
bathing
desires
 lovers
moaning
transfixed
because you make me
 because you make me
come
here
 now
bathe me

Aquí

burning
burning
what is my name?
come
 Here
Now
soothe my thirst
drink from the fountain
 of eternal bliss
ven
Nirvana
 electric
 currents
Kundalini

relics of desires
eternal
bathe me

Aquí

ven
loose the fears
loose yourself
call
call me
call my name
burning
bliss
burning
wanting
more
again
come
again
call
call my name
the oldest desire in the world
take me once more
make me scream
howl
squirm
tremble
again.

 # 1

Cuanta belleza en el amanecer
Cuanta hermosura en la creación
Y sentir que soy parte de ella
Soy
Un ingrediente y una totalidad
Soy una célula y una galaxia
Soy el sol
Y la nube fría del viento de huracán
Soy la paloma volando sobre el arco iris
Soy la montaña maciza
 y suavemente ondulada
Soy el río dulce que
Cabalga hacia el mar
Soy creación eterna
En el umbral de la nada
Acariciando la bendición gloriosa
Del amor maternal.

#2

Love comes in small doses
In soft murmurs
And whispers of hope
Everyday
Every hour
Every minute
Every second
Breathing is a blessing
Life is a wonderful mystery
And
Love is spelled with the scent of jasmine
And amapolas.

#3

Cabalgata agonizante
Bravura de mar sofocante
Rapaz deseo de tu piel
De tu risa
 Y agonía
Requiebra el riachuelo
De esperanzas secas
Amado mío
Salpica el deseo infinito
De tenerte
De tocarte
De poder acariciarte
Enciende querubines
Mi Amado
Cabalga esta pasión
De fuego eterno.

Millennium

Tantos años
De acá para allá
Tantos años de allá para acá
Va Y ven
Va y ven
 Van
Las olas
Las olas
Escuchan
El murmullo del cinsonte
El viento de la tormenta
1898
De allá para acá
De acá para allá
Las olas
Las olas
Escuchan
La tormenta.

El Norte

All you dream is of making it there
All you dream is of making it here
Iam here not there
Not where the sun burn your skin and you dream in spanish
and is not yet spanglish is not English but you want to be
here
where the winter freezes your heart but at the same time
free your soul
how is that?
And you dream of going back and you dream of retiring
fast and then
everything will be back to the way it was, yes, but how?
And each day you go about life
wake up in the morning rain or shine because that is the
American way .

No excuses or you don't have a job. No lateness or you
wont have a job.
No dreams because then you will want to live.
And so you continue to save for your annual trip to see the
family
and you wonder ...how it happened?
And you wonder about your decision to come here or there

because you feel that you don't belong anywhere.

And now
how is that ?

EL CARRO BOTE

I couldn't believe it when I heard it on the radio.
Again the Cubans came up with another car -boat.
I mean, these people drove a car in the middle of the
Caribbean sea.
Driving a car in the middle of the sea?
They arrived in Florida
and
the Coast Guard send them back home
On an airplane.

Other Stories

#1
Hmmm Yo vine aquí pa'trabajar
Y estoy trabajando.

#2
What the...!
My parents came here when I was young.
They both worked hard
Mami en la fábrica y papi lavando platos Y de
conserje.
Now Iam completing a two year degree in a
community college.
That is all I can afford
My parents
came searching a dream
And now what?

#3
Y qué?
Nosotros no somos los Únicos que venimos
Aquí !
Yo veo irlandeses, Africanos, Rusos,
Alemanes, Franceses, Italians, Chinos
Y Los de allá arriba de Canada!
Siempre la Cogen con Nosotros
Será que no les gusta el ¿Español?

#4

Oye
 what about the Puerto Ricans?
They keep coming back and forth
Back and forth

Mira que tienen to' el Bronx y el barrio

Algunos se escaparon pa' long island y staten island
tratando de pasar por blanquitos.
Ahora están tos en Orlando y en Delaware.
Ellos no tiene Green card.
La suerte de esos malditos, no necesitan la green
card.

#5
Si te preguntan de donde son
Ustedes dicen que son americanas.

 Nosotros somos Puertorriqueños.

#6
Well, the last time I heard, the real Americans are in
concentration camps called reservations.

#7
Oh, please, all this bull about immigrants. What about
the ones that came in the Mayflower? They were
immigrants too!

#8
Does anybody have a clue about how the US
expanded to the west? Really do you know?
Let me give you a clue, it was not John Wayne.
First they declared war on the Indians after basically
killing them all up.

and then... they fought the Mexicans and won.
That is why the United States took over what is
now,Arizona,New Mexico, California. You get it? It is
all about war. A few years from Now,we might be
speaking Mandarin.

#9
Dad I thought that this was a Japanese restaurant.
Yes, my dear.
Soooooooo, what is that Mexican
 doing in the kitchen?

#10

*The statue of Liberty is a gift from France... I guess
that she is also an immigrant.*

#11
*Rename the Puerto Rican Day Parade
The only day we believe in ourselves.*

#12

Writers Retreat

Take all the MFA writing artists
Ask them to live in East New York, El Barrio, Loisaida
Harlem and the South Bronx
Now they can learn to create Art.

La Noche de Fuentes

Hoy conocí a Carlos Fuentes
En una noche de invierno
y a escondidas
en una cueva intelectual
noche fría del holocausto norteño
Suspire sus palabras
Estaba firmando libros
mas yo no tenía ninguno de sus obras majestuosas
conmigo
me compre una edición en ingles
SACRILEGIO
Jamás yo leeré a Fuentes en Ingles
Pero quería verlo nuevamente
y compre un libro en ingles
como buena nuyorkina
hice la fila
mirando a mercaderes docenas
de libros
No aprecian la maravilla de la palabra
mana de vida
suspiro eterno
Al llegar me mira
y para mi sorpresa
entonamos una breve conversación
le dije háblame en español
me miro y me dio un piropo
Carlos Fuentes me dio un piropo
con sus manos
con su mirada
y con la expresión de sus ojos juguetones
Que noche perfecta
en la soledad
de la ciudad de hierro
en la noche obscura de un frio infernal
Carlos Fuentes me hizo suspirar
y sonar en la magia ancestral
de nuestro idioma materno.

SOFRITO

We are
   Mezcla caliente
      Cilantro
     Pimientos y ajos
   cortando
        cut
        cortando
        cut
     cebolla y ajicitos
cortando cut
cortando cut
reds
   greens
yellows
     whites
  blacks
&
  browns
machacando en el pilón
experiences
simmering
calentando en la sartén
   new flavors

cortando   cut
cortando cut
Comiendo en El Bronx,
Latinos en Nuyol
But is not Latin
There is no LatinO Language
Only an umbilical cord of passion and desires
We are

69

ancient &
         modern
Indians and Blacks straight from the motherland
senses on fire
 desires
and the sudden pleasure of
Ahhh
Hmmm
             DeliciouS
       spicy
         Iam not use to this blend
         Iam not used to this taste
     Simmering
despacito
        many colors
     cortando
       cut
cortando cut
we are putting the Bang in the bland

Cortando
  Cut
Cortando cut
Calentando
    Despacito
Ay   que   ricoOOOOOOOO
Aqui estamos
 En el frio
      Warming the heart of
          a nation
that lives in the
 past
cortando cut
cortando cut
cortando cut

we are
Spanish
   English
Spanglish
 A new language born
In farms
Sweat shops
Kitchens
Construction sites
Y
Las calles
 el arduo sudor
Perfuma nuestra existencia

  Many nations in one
Conquistadores y conquistados
Alforja del nuevo ser
 historia y pasión
Cortando
Cut
Cortando
Cut

La raza cósmica
Somos

       El Sofrito.

Denial

No
Because
because
   You
Because you

You you you you

you
   Know

Y ou Know
You know

It's not fair
because
   You know

T hat
to know
to know
Means that

No no no no no no
Iam

N aked

I n
Secure
Insecure
N aked
No
bound
Boundaries

W alls
Pretending
to Be

B ut

Iam not
Because
Because
You know

It h urts

And i
I
don't know
Because
  I I I ii I

I am

S

C

A

R

Ed

Despertando

I
Am
In
A
Cocoon

I
Am
A
Shadow
Of
A new
Reality

Voices
Circle
My heart

Ancestral
Rhythms
Moving

Chanting
Dreaming
Singing
Birthing

Feel me
Iam
Here
Now

Breathing
Creating
Webbing

Iam
One
completa
One
Sin fronteras
One
In speckles of cosmic dust
Breathing creation

Con mis manos
Con mi espera
En lazos de jazmín y hiedra
One
En la alforja
Y el morivivi
One
En el rio grande
Y la arena caliente arropando las palmeras
One
En las memorias del Atlántico
One
En el futuro incierto
One
En la canción sencilla
One
Forever

Aquí

Calladita
Creando telarañas en mis cicatrices
One

En el candomble y la plena
One
Para siempre
Eterna.

ABOUT THE AUTHOR

Carmen Bardeguez-Brown is a poet and educator from Puerto Rico. She migrated to the United States in 1984 courtesy of American Airlines and the colonial quid pro quo status. Although a poet since she can remembered, she became a member of the spoken word/poetry scene that took place in the early 1990s at the Nuyorican Poets Cafe. She was a member of Steve Cannon and Bob Holman "Stoop" Writing workshop.

Her work was showcase in the documentary: Latino Poets in the United States. an award documentary filmed and produced by Ray Santiesteban that showcase her among other founding members of the Nuyorican Poets movement such as Pedro Pietri and Willie Perdomo. She has been feature many times at The Nuyorican Poets Café, The Fez, Mad Alex Foundation, Smoke, The Soho Arts Festival, Long wood Gallery, The Kitchen, La Casa Azul, New Years Alternative Poetry Marathon 2013 and 2014. The Boricua College Poetry Series curated by Myrna Nieves, The Capicu Cultural Series, The New York Poetry Festival at Governors Island, The Bowery Poetry Club,Sarah Lawrence College Poetry Reading series and many other venues in the tri-state area.

Some of her work has been performed by Felipe Luciano's Poets's Choir, Butch Morris Conduction series #27 performed at The Whitney Museum and Art in Progress Cantieri Del Contemporaneo at Cosenza Italy; the performance interpretation can be seen in You Tube. The Caribbean Cultural Theater panel and poetry reading June 2013 and Afro Latino writers panel and poetry reading at Medgar Evers College.

Her work has been published by magazines such as: Tribes, Long Shot, Fuse, School Voices, recently interview and feature in the on line radio show No Boarders Poetry Radio, Rutgers Gallery at New Brunswick,Anthology: Aloud Voices from the Nuyorican, Phatitude Cultural Magazine 2012, Woman Writers in Bloom on line magazine, La Pluma y La Tinta Anthology edited by Raquel Penzo, Nuyorican Poets Writers Vol.1 edited by Dr. Nancy Mercado, Xanath Caraza 2015 Poetry Blog. Four of her poems were selected for the forthcoming Afrolatino poetry anthology to be published by Arte Publico press in 2016.

She produced a poetry cd and book title: " Straight From the Drum". A collection of poems that encapsulate her Afro Caribbean poetic rhythm. Her poetry book Straight from the Drums: Al Ritmo del Tambor could be purchased in Amazon, Barnes and Nobles or a bookstore near you. You could follow her blog at cbbpoetry@tumblr.com. For more information or if you want to invite her to read her work send her an email at cbbpoetry@gmail.com

COMMENTS

Foreward is forewarned is forearmed and two legged too. Be forewarned that this book is for the dancers. Whether they drop on the one or the two, it is the alchemy of clave and comma, punto and period This book you must carry as a drum, it is the answer to the question, "¿A dónde va?" To tambor. It has your part in the orchestration of culture, tradition, and all human aspirations. These are the reflection of the culture left behind at the port of entry at the birthing pains of a syncopations in waiting. This book is a long overdue tome from CBB.

> "Rumbanbeame (From "Senora")
> Del dream
> Tun tun"

Carmen BB sings these pages then lays them out for the eye to rapid eye movement, "sueños" They are maps to the ancient steps and steppes that she has chanted on a succession of open mics open to sainted rhythms straight from the pyramids of and underground poetic benbes. The saints have marched in and left none wanting. The paper Carmen Bardeguez-Brown has attached here is the cuero fastened to trans Caribbean voyages in hollowed and allowed living tree played to announce birth and death and new ages coming. There is no poem in this book that does not declare itself a love poem. Love is harsh and ironic too, even when she dances.

"You need to taste memories of salt and water blood and chains" writes Carmen Bardeguez in the poem "Rememberance", "to understand". The calls for remembering, recognition, awareness, love and fancy are all the things that spring from the memories and dance with a joy defiant and insistent in defiance in these poems. Even when they address the savage unresolved and ironic of human history; "Invested in centuries of illusions Repressed sperms crucify vaginas" Bardeguez reigns in all bitterness while exploring the cosmic joke of such affairs. There is no indicting, just observations. You must play your part in the rhythm.

"Orischas
Swirl Ache
Asfalto bembeando
Candomble candoneando
Sirenas
Danceando
Los suenos"

You can go to the dance and come home draped in the rhythms of saints or tricksters, Elegba greets you at the turn of each page. Carmen Bardeguez-Brown has fashioned these poems in the course of a lifetime of cultural immigration across two continents or three and the small islands in their midsts.

As an educator and an image fashioner, Bardeguez-Brown is in the forefront of even the advance guards. She has worked this formula where ever poetry sought and has had a foothold. These are the observation of a lifetime of expression---there is the word and the word was with all intent on hearing These poems are still telling but never still. You have been invited to a dance, you have been invited to dance at the communion of the saints, to spring forward, "jump back and do the Camel Walk". You need only these dancing phrases words. Read freely.

"LOVE POEMS IN DANCE STEPS WRITTEN
IN THE DUST OF SWEET CLAY EARTH"
Keith Roach

EDITOR'S NOTE

In the editing of this book we have respected the punctuation, font, language and other choices made by the author in her manuscript. We believe that Carmen's poetry is about rhythm and that the format of her writing is part of her aesthetic sound.

Miguel López Lemus

Publisher

Pandora lobo estepario Productions™
http://www.loboestepario.com/press
Chicago/Oaxaca

Front Cover Art:
by: Yolanda Velazquez Velez
Back cover photo:
Miguel López Lemus

Editor: Miguel López Lemus©

www.ingramcontent.com/pod-product-compliance
Lightning Source LLC
Chambersburg PA
CBHW032146040426
42449CB00005B/415